AF425663

ECHOES FROM THE DIVINE

An Anthology of Poems on the Qur'an

ECHOES FROM THE DIVINE
An Anthology of Poems on the Qur'an

Edited by:

Sara Farhat, Ahmed Ayoub, Tehreem Khalid,
Eiman Bushra, Mariam Ali & Sara Bawany

Foreword by:
Imam Dr. Khalid Shahu

Copyright © 2026 by House of Amal
Foreword © 2026 Imam Dr. Khalid Shahu

First Edition. All rights reserved.

Each contributor to this anthology retains the copyright to their own individual work. Permission to reproduce or distribute any material in this anthology must be obtained directly from the respective author or artist.

No part of this publication may be reproduced, distributed, or transmitted in any form or by any means, including digital, without the prior written permission of the copyright holder, except for brief quotations used in critical reviews or educational purposes, in accordance with fair use guidelines.

Cover artwork by Agija M., "Light", used with permission. For more information, visit www.instagram.com/aquarellmuslimah

100% of the proceeds of this book will go to Islam in Prison (www.islaminprison.org), a division of Al-Furqaan Foundation (www.furqaan.org), a non-profit organization dedicated to delivering the message of the Qur'an to those who are incarcerated.

For more information on House of Amal, please visit www.houseofamal.co and www.instagram.com/house.of.amal

Publisher: House of Amal
ISBN: 979-8-9918907-3-1
Printed in The United States of America

بِسْمِ ٱللَّهِ الرَّحْمَٰنِ الرَّحِيمِ

Authors' Note:

As this book contains text from the Qur'an in both its content and its cover, we kindly recommend that our esteemed readers treat it with the appropriate respect and avoid placing it in locations where the sanctity of the Qur'an may not be observed.

TABLE OF CONTENTS

INTRODUCTION

Iqra.

The first command reverberated by the walls of Cave Hira: *Read.*

Our beloved Prophet ﷺ, the unlettered, replied, "I am not one who reads," a statement that is echoed by us today but for different reasons. Our Qur'ans lay closed on shelves of dust not because of illiteracy but because of the distractions of the dunya, the barriers we have built in our minds: the language is too difficult, and the depth seemingly beyond our grasp to comprehend. We let it sit on the shelf, missing out on the double reward promised for the struggle of reading the Holy Book. We forget our Lord is Al-Wadud (The Most Loving), Al Hadi (The Guide)—the One who doesn't reward us for our fluency or speed of reading, but rather rewards us for our efforts, honoring the struggle itself. He encourages us to read regardless because the struggle is more valuable than the ease.

"Read! And your Lord is the Most Generous." (Qur'an 96:3)

This verse from Surah Al-'Alaq, the first Surah revealed, continues with, "Who taught by the pen." (96:4) Iqra and the pen. The first command and the first created thing, presented together in the first Surah revealed. Iqra and the pen. The two pillars of knowledge, together from the very beginning. Yet so often, we separate them. We write, but we don't read to replenish our writer's reservoir. We read, but we don't write our reflections, our ponderings, our gained knowledge. Severing the bond between writing and reading.

At House of Amal, we believe that to be a writer, one *must* read. We believe writing is a spiritual practice, the art of listening to what the Divine is conveying to you, through you. There is no better way to practice this art than to read the very words of Allah delivered by the lips of an angel.

The idea for this Qur'an Anthology, comprising 30 poems for the 30 ajza', was planted in Ramadan, the month of the Qur'an, the month the verses of Iqra descended from the heavens to earth. The command—Iqra—is our inheritance. At House of Amal, we seek to mend the sacred bond between reading and writing and that is why this project was sown. Its purpose is to reunite the pen and Iqra within ourselves, as presented in the first Surah revealed. This project was an invitation for creatives to build a bond with the Qur'an, to not only read it, but to pick up our pens as well. To use them to etch our findings and our contemplations onto our pages. For the pen and the divine pages weaved together in creative expression to allow a meaningful and stronger connection to the Qur'an, so that our reply to Iqra is, "I *am* one who reads."

The Qur'an is truly a gift, and everyone should have access to it. Alhamdulillah, we are grateful to say that 100% of the proceeds from this anthology are going to Islam in Prison via Al-Furqaan Foundation, an organization which sends copies of the Qur'an to incarcerated individuals and foster access to its teachings.

We strive for the noor of these words to permeate through every space and be a source of hope and light.

Here, within these pages is a reflection of our love for the pen and for engaging in Iqra.

Sara Farhat
House of Amal
Content Director

FOREWORD

In the name of Allah, the All-Merciful, the All-Compassionate. Peace and blessings be upon His Beloved Messenger ﷺ, his family, his progeny, his companions, and his followers until the Day of Resurrection.

In every generation, the Qur'an descends anew—not in its text, for that is *mahfūz*, safeguarded by the Divine—but in meaning, in encounter, in hearts awakened and souls stirred. This book, comprising thirty poems in homage to the thirty *ajzā'* of the Qur'an, is one such descent. It is a quiet yet resonant act of devotion, reflection, and reclamation—a testament to the enduring intimacy between revelation and the receptive heart.

In a world increasingly fragmented by noise and distraction—where identity is flattened and faith tested, where sacred speech is often drowned out by the clamor of forgetting—projects like this are of profound importance. They become vessels of renewal. They remind us that the Qur'an is not a relic to be revered from afar, but a living voice calling us near. They offer Muslim voices a space to reimagine sacred language in forms both ancient and unfolding.

When the spirit of faith takes on the mantle of literature—expressing itself through poetry, wisdom, parables, sincere advocacy, eloquent words, memorable sayings, or clever dramatization—gentle exhortation can reach the hearts of people with quiet power. It can bring awareness to the plight of the oppressed, inspire love for the Islamic way of life, critique the corruption of ignorance, awaken in Muslims the spirit of strength and struggle, and renew their commitment to carrying the divine message and building a model society—one that is compassionate to humanity, merciful to all creation, and fiercely devoted to justice.

The poetic word can heal and confront, soften and sharpen, elevate and ground. Poetry has long served as the vessel for the soul's deepest longings. And the Qur'an, too, arrived not only as law and guidance but as rhythm, as beauty, as overwhelming eloquence. It came not as prose, but as luminous speech—*Tajwīd* and *Tartīl*. Verses cascading like waves, meanings unfolding like petals. It silenced desert poets, gave dignity to the enslaved, and stilled the tongues of the most eloquent. It is no coincidence that the Final Messenger ﷺ was sent to a culture steeped in verse: revelation came in a language that pierced the soul.

This anthology stands humbly in that tradition—not to rival, but to respond. Each poem is a devotional murmur, a contemplative echo, a gesture of nearness. It does not seek to explain the Qur'an, but to sit with it. To ask it questions. To be questioned by it. And, perhaps most importantly, to be transformed through it.

Indeed, poetry becomes a *miḥrāb* of contemplation—a turning of the inner self toward the Divine. And in turning to the Qur'an, we turn to the very axis of meaning. As Sayyidunā 'Alī (may Allah ennoble his face) once recounted:

"Indeed, I heard Allah's Messenger ﷺ say: 'Dissension will certainly arise.' I ('Alī) then asked, 'What is the way to avoid it, O Messenger of Allah?' He ﷺ replied: 'The way is Allah's Book, for it contains information about what came before you, news of what will come after you, and judgment regarding what occurs among you. It is the criterion that distinguishes between truth and falsehood. Whoever abandons it out of arrogance, Allah will humble him; and whoever seeks guidance elsewhere, Allah will misguide him. It is Allah's strong rope, the wise reminder, and the straight path. Desires do not corrupt it, tongues do not confuse it, and it does not wear out from repeated recitation. Its wonders never cease, and the scholars never tire of its study. It is that about which the jinn said:
"Indeed, we have heard a wondrous Qur'an, which guides to what is
right, and we have believed in it." (Qur'an, Surah Jinn 72:1–2).

Whoever speaks according to it speaks the truth; whoever acts upon it is rewarded; whoever judges by it is just; and whoever invites others to it is guided to the straight path.'" (Narrated by al-Tirmidhī and al-Dārimī)

Another noble companion, 'Abdullāh ibn Mas'ūd (may Allah be pleased with him), emphasized how the Messenger of Allah ﷺ invited us to explore the treasures of the Qur'an when he said:

"This Qur'an is Allah's invitation to us. So, learn from it as much as you can. It is the Rope of Allah, the clear Light, and a beneficial Healing. It is a protection for the one who clings to it and a rescue for the one who follows it. It is never crooked that it should need straightening, and it never deviates that it should be blamed. Its wonders never cease, and it never wears out with repetition." (Narrated by al-Hākim)

Likewise, Anas (may Allah be pleased with him) reported that the Messenger of Allah ﷺ said:

"The Qur'an is a wealth after which there is no poverty, nor is there a better wealth." (Narrated by Abū Ya'lā)

What these three hadiths—and many others—proclaim with radiant clarity, this anthology seeks to echo with reverent creativity: that the Qur'an is not only *hukm* (judgment) and *bayān* (clarification), but *'ajab*—a source of abiding wonder. Its guidance is unerring; its beauty, inexhaustible. Its wonders truly never cease. And to approach it through poetry is not to dilute its majesty, but to behold it with the trembling awe of the inspired.

Each poem in this collection is a gesture—a listening ear, a whisper of love, a pause between verses. It is an invitation to return to the Book not only with the intellect, but with the imagination, the longing, the inward ache that seeks to be led. These thirty poems do not presume to interpret the Qur'an, but to witness it—to reflect its light in the language of yearning. To become, in their own small way, part of the living echo of revelation.

May these thirty poems serve as lanterns along that path.

May they illuminate something of the Divine Light found in each *juz'*.

May they awaken in every reader the timeless ache to draw nearer to the One who spoke.

And may Allah reward House of Amal's project and its founders and pioneers for initiating such a beautiful and fruitful endeavor.

Imam Dr. Khalid Shahu

BISMILLAH AL-RAHMAN AL-RAHEEM

Tehreem Khalid

Alhamdulillah, we recite—praise the Lord of seven heavens
who breathed life into our mould, sent words of nourishment

with elif begins this revelation—a blueprint for those seeking,
weaving lessons of guidance entwined with great wisdom

each surah soaked in mercy, every ayah stands witness,
a divine gift descended: so we may ponder, we may listen

when the why's become burdensome, prayers go unanswered;
the answer remained unopened in Al-Shifa sitting on a shelf

as life depletes our hearts of taqwa, the rhymeful verses
rush through our vessels renewing the souls rhythm

when our hearts go astray, when our life's in dismay,
dua'as come to rescue—as do tales of God's most beloved

miracles upon miracles revealed to the holy prophet ﷺ
every letter a miracle—its preservation too, a miracle

every word on our tongues enriches our akhirah like seeds,
mercy filling empty scars, awaiting the warmth of spring

so we open it to learn about stories of past and present,
Bismillah, always, the Most Beneficent, the Most Merciful

Alhamdulillah, we repeat, for this book of reminders
that accompanies weak hearts and weary souls of an-nas

BLISSFUL PATIENCE
Abdulrahman Taiwo Adedayo

Heart wrenching—hope giving—so was the tale told
by He whose light shan't dim nor fold:
That of a father whose son was torn amiss,
yet clung to faith in the Exalted with bliss.

Of the return of his beloved, he stood in certainty
at times where the odds were bleak in fragility.
Then by divine decree, returned his son—the Azeez,
bearing comfort he brought but peace and ease.

So does the Omnipotent bless the patient,
with grace divine and love ever radiant.
He mends the broken heart once torn and worn,
and bestows light in the faithful, a heart reborn.

TRIBUTE TO THE SOLE COMPANION

Umar Latif

The glass of the mirror only reflects light
But you chased away the darkness within
I lost my wings and you taught me flight
Became my deepest friend, my closest kin

In the vermilion skies of youthful dawn
I sought healing not knowing it was you
That nursed me as a doe does her fawn
Or as the daisy is by fresh fallen dew

I was blissful, misled from the reality
Which you defined in numbing clarity
That of humans and fated mortality
The condition imposed of our finality

Meaningless were my silent supplications
Made by old habit, formed without essence
I was like one in your stern repudiations
Engulfed, entrapped in this evanescence

My tutor, leader, guide and mentor
This poem, for The Poem, I compose
My circumference and my center
My being and that which I enclose

Evident for its verities, Al-Burhan,
Surpassing all poetries, Al-Bayan,
Discerning our dualities, Al-Furqan,
All are names for but one, Al-Qur'an

AMĀNAH
Fatima ElKalay

إِنَّا عَرَضْنَا ٱلْأَمَانَةَ عَلَى ٱلسَّمَـٰوَٰتِ وَٱلْأَرْضِ وَٱلْجِبَالِ فَأَبَيْنَ أَن يَحْمِلْنَهَا وَأَشْفَقْنَ مِنْهَا وَحَمَلَهَا ٱلْإِنسَـٰنُ ۖ إِنَّهُ كَانَ ظَلُومًا جَهُولاً.

"Indeed, We offered the trust to the heavens and the earth and the mountains, but they [all] declined to bear it, being fearful of it. But humanity assumed it, [for] they are truly wrongful [to themselves] and ignorant [of the consequences.]"
- Qur'an, Surah Al-Ahzab 33:72

The sun arrives, precise, unmoaning;
we meet her light like querulous moles,
preferring deeper sleep.
We rise, at last,
to parse the syllables of another day,
beneath a sky wise to decline.

Here we are: cold coffee, traffic,
bills washed white by a floral spritzer
in a crossover.
Then night crosses over,
claims the sun's scroll
and ingests us.

We weigh our losses and our blessings,
disrobe tired bodies:
a contract we signed,
too deaf to grasp the other language,
or know
what we carry.

Who would be eager
to carry the weight for mountains,
the price that chained us
to free will?

We undo ourselves and each other,
with knives in our words, words
in our knives. We bleed
our brothers into soil
that bore the wound it never chose.

We wade our foolish minds
through mile-high grain,
see nothing but the husked space
between our eyes,
tread paths that never come again,
through the feather and dust
of our entrusted things.

Do we not see
how the vast sky encircling us
bows its head,
tucks in the world,
tent-taut and unflawed?
How the sun bends corners out of sight,
how the earth
dies to birth its seasons
to Greater wisdom and command?

Do we not see,
do we not see—

but we, so small
said our small yes
to sleep and bury deep,
soak in bitter blood,
carry, and carry it all.

We broke the land and seas.

A small yes rises to His Dominion:
the weight of mountains
descends.

IRENIC IRIDESCENCE

Ikram Bouhedda

One end held by the salik:

Clouds of hearts weighed by molecules of the innate veils.
At dismantle, the nafs elevates humble and frail—
His siraj deflects lights in hues for the mind's avail.

Calming ripples of soft blues
Infinite ink of His words reflects self-hues.

Purity paves groves of green
Heights of purity, unseen.

Healing tapestries of yellows
To guide anxiety's echoes.

Set? Rise? Orange
Wird syringe.

Wudd through veins of red
From our heart to His mercy, mawada is spread.

Deflection in the adornment of landscape's effect.
A steganographic symbolism of introspect.
Shunning, in the promise, every dhalala and halak.

:Other end held by our Malik.

"ARE YOU QUR'AN?"

Mahmoodulhasan Bhaiyat

In between kicks, the new neighbor's son smiles
        as he sees me and I say salam.

He asks me, too young to know all the right words,
        "Are you Qur'an?" With a grin, I say,
        "Yes, I am Qur'an." I am all thirty ajzaa' memorized—
        but am I even thirty ayaat realized?

I wonder how he knew when he doesn't even know
        my name, both of us familiar only by face;
        I figure he figured from my form-fitted thawb,
        buttons blinging and collar tight against my throat.

I kick the soccer ball away from his little brother's
        feet and feign to play for a couple more fakes before
        I say salam and walk the remaining way home.

In their little legged league, I guess I'm the monolithic
        mascot now, and the worst part is, if you look the part,
        you gotta play the part too.

I am now the friendly neighborhood Qur'an,
        not a possibly faulty nogginal node of a divinely
        distributed ledger, but the very kitaab itself—
        half-time or not, whenever I'm spotted, "I am Qur'an."

THE INK AND THE ECHO
Hassan Hakim

O wanderer in the valley of thought,
you speak of free will as if it is a lantern without oil,
as if the night does not swallow the blind traveler whole.
You say, "Common sense is enough."
But whose common sense? Yours? Mine?
The tyrant who drinks blood as if it is milk?
The merchant who sells heavy weights with deceit?
The mother who weeps over a child taught falsehood as truth?

Oh soul, do you not see?
Truth is not woven from the strings of men's opinions,
for men are like shifting dunes,
changing with every passing wind.

And the One who shaped your hands,
who measured the distance from your breath to the stars,
does not leave you lost in the gray.
He does not say, "Guess the road."
He says, "And We revealed to you the Reminder
so that you may explain to the people
what was sent down to them…" [1]

If the lantern of free will were enough,
why do men build towers upon sinking sand?
Why do they carve idols
from the clay of their own egos?
No, the ink of Revelation is not in vain.
The One who wrote the stars has already written the map.

O seeker of clarity, you say,
"My answers find me. The Qur'an speaks to my soul.
A verse arrives when I need it most."

---

[1] Qur'an, Surah An-Nahl, 16:44

And indeed, that is a mercy from the Most High.
But what of the one who reads with trembling hands in darkness?
What of the one who finds a verse and twists it like a blade
to fit the mold of his own desire?

You are a pearl in the ocean, but do not forget—
an ocean without a governing pull is chaos without shore.

And so the Prophet ﷺ was sent
not only to recite, but to explain,
not only to deliver, but to demonstrate,
not only to speak, but to live the ink upon the scroll.

Was it not said,
"And We have not revealed to you the Book except
that you may explain to them that wherein they differ…" [2]

A man may drink water from his hands,
but a cup was given so that he may drink without spilling.
A man may try to walk alone,
but a guide was sent so that he does not lose his way.

Oh soul, do you not see?
The Qur'an is the water.
The Prophet ﷺ is the cup.
The Qur'an is the road.
The Prophet ﷺ is the guide.

If Allah willed, He would have left prayer without form,
fasting without rules, justice without law.
But He, in His mercy, did not leave the river without banks,
nor the heart without a rhythm to beat itself toward balance.

The Qur'an is a light,
but a light in the hands of the blind is nothing but a weight.

---

[2] Qur'an, Surah An-Nahl, 16:64

A verse in the hands of a seeker
is a sword sharpened by truth.
A verse in the hands of a tyrant
is a weapon stained with his own reflection.

So tell me, O thinker, if your way were the only way,
why do men argue over the same verse?
Why does one see mercy while another sees war?
Why does one see freedom while another builds chains?

Because the Qur'an is vast.
And the Prophet ﷺ is the key.
Because the Qur'an is an ocean,
and the Prophet ﷺ is the boat.

O lovers of simplicity,
do not mistake structure for oppression,
nor guidance for control.
The tree does not call the soil its captor.
The moon does not curse the gravity that holds it.
For in that balance is the harmony of the Divine.

"Obey Allah and obey the Messenger…" [3]
This is not two paths, but one road.
Not two commands, but one voice.
So drink from the well, but do not reject the bucket.
Read the Book, but do not discard the one who lived within its ink.
For he was not merely a scribe, but the walking Qur'an.

And when the world whispers in your ear
to trust only yourself, remember,
even the brightest stars still bow to the orbit set by their Creator.

And so must we.

---

[3] Qur'an, Surah An-Nisa, 4:59

"YOUR GOD LETS CHILDREN DIE?"

Zana Ishak

They ask,
How can we love a God
who lets children die?
As if He owes an answer
to those who traded truth for convenience.
As if their eyes ever wept
before dead children
became a debating point.

They ask,
What kind of God allows suffering?
The kind we have always known.
The One who let Fir'awn build his empire
and still split the sea like silk.
The One who never promised a life without fire
but that He is with us in it.
"O fire! Be cool and safe for Abraham!" [4]
The One who let Maryam cry for death
then rained dates upon her.
"Do not grieve!" [5]
The One who let Nuh watch
as the waters overwhelmed his son, then said,
"Disembark with our peace and blessings on you." [6]

They ask,
If God is real, why do people starve?
As if hunger proves absence.
As if wealth proves approval.
They hoard what was meant to be shared,
sell the bombs that make orphans,

---

[4] Qur'an, Surah Al-Anbiya, 21:68
[5] Qur'an, Surah Maryam, 19:24
[6] Qur'an, Surah Hud, 11:48

stockpile grains while children waste away.
Then interrogate God.

They ask,
When will your Lord help?
As if suffering is a verdict.
As if *when* is a language
God agreed to speak.

"Indeed, the help of Allah is near."[7]
You hear near
and reach for a clock
a scale
a calendar.

But it is not until the tyrant has done
everything evil can do.
It is not until the dust settles,
and faith prevails over fear.

Or not even then.
The knowledge was never ours.
Time answers to Him.

They keep asking God
to answer for what people do.
As if evil doesn't walk on human feet.
As if evil wasn't something
being chosen again and again.
As if galaxies written into being
somehow erased accountability.

Even the angels knew:
Will You place upon the earth one who sheds blood?
and He answered:

---

[7] Qur'an, Surah Al-Baqarah, 2:214

I know what you know not. [8]
So no,
we won't reduce the Divine
to diagrams and debates.

But if they must have proof,
say it's:

In every tyrant who fell.
In the blade that did not harm.
In the spring that gushed and still flows.
In the belly of a whale that held.
In the dark well that became a passage.
In every mother who still names her child 'hope'.
In foreheads on the ground
while the sky collapses.

And when the reckoning comes—
and it will—
No argument survives Him.
No logic.
No eloquence.
No escape.

"Say: Your Lord is Infinite in Mercy—
but His punishment will not be averted
from the wrongdoing people." [9]

---

[8] Qur'an, Surah Al-Baqarah, 2:30
[9] Qur'an, Surah Al-An'am, 6:147

WHEN YOU ARE BROKEN
Sumayyah Hussein

The verses
hit
differently
when you
are
broken.

When your heart is shredded
with a million
little rips—frayed
by the small incisions
of everyday offenses—
or torn straight through
with gaping
holes—gashes
from the calamities
that bring you to your knees—
the words flow over them,
the rips and the holes,
like water on parched soil.

When you are
broken,
there is no comfort to be had
from the world—not so alluring anymore—
its colors fading into black,
its flavors
to ash,
its persuasive whispers
to meaningless static.

When you are
broken,
all you crave

are the words you need to hear,
that fill the rips and the holes,
that carry comfort,
truth,
and the reality—not so bitter, after all—
that you are nothing
without Him.

'YOU WOULD KILL YOURSELF WITH GRIEF' [10]

Warren Clementson

A medium-sized guilt occupies my lungs

weighs down my diaphragm.

I hear you praised by the congregation;

rather than echo their sentiment

I cough myself into an apprehensive trance.

My feet are dragged towards your mother's tongue

and in rushing through life's path

thorns stab away at my ears;

now all I hear is blood

dripping on concrete.

For everything I knew of you

I never knew what you wanted to say.

---

[10] Qur'an, Surah Al-Kahf, 18:6

BELIEVING IN THE UNSEEN

Hajera Khaja

Age 16:

I wake up
in the middle of the night, turn on the desk lamp
open the green hardcover, begin at the beginning

*This is the Scripture in which there is no doubt, containing guidance for those who
are mindful of God, who believe in the unseen.* [11]

Somewhere along the troubles of being a teenager,
running into friends, crushes,
university applications,
I abandon the waking
the book left unopened, dark nights with
no halo
of light above my head
no urgency
for guidance.

Age 21:

Driving through silent streets, I want to catch
laylatul qadr
A minaret lit up green rises in the distance
I have a pocket Qur'an and I want to follow along
but I am late
I don't know where the imam is
in his recitation
I step out of the car, into the inky night
a hoarse voice tumbles out of the speakers
reciting verses
I had paused

---

[11] Qur'an, Surah Al-Baqarah, 2:2-3

at the same evening

*For men and women who are devoted to God—believing men and women,
obedient men and women, truthful men and women, steadfast men and women,
humble men and women, charitable men and women, fasting men and women,
chaste men and women, men and women who remember God often, God has
prepared forgiveness and a rich reward.* [12]

Age 27:

I am walking away without
having prayed
in the rawdah, a garden
from the gardens of paradise
in the city of
the Prophet, the city of
light, the city of
miracles

Instead of a miracle, I get
elbows sticking into my sides
bodies pushing
from the back and from the front and from the left and from the
right
and it feels like the dua I make has been
blocked
*[place behind me light and in front of me light and above me light
and beneath me light]*
no light for me
in the city of light

The walk of shame
back to my hotel room, my shadow
taunts,
this is written for me because I am a woman.

---

[12] Qur'an, Surah Al-Ahzab, 33:35

At fajr, light cracks the sky
open, shadows
                    recede
The Imam recites verses revealed in response
to another woman's question,
my question:

*For men and women who are devoted to God- believing men and women, obedient
men and women, truthful men and women, steadfast men and women, humble
men and women, charitable men and women, fasting men and women, chaste men
and women, men and women who remember God often, God has prepared
forgiveness and a rich reward.* [13]

Age 39:

I am still at war
with myself
sitting in a class with Sheikha Iesha Prime

Let me tell you about Khawla, she says.

*God has heard the words of the woman who disputed with you [Prophet] about
her husband and complained to God: God has heard what you both had to say.
He is all hearing, all seeing.* [14]

The punishment
does not match the crime—
freeing a slave
fasting for two months
feeding sixty needy people—
That is how valuable your emotional safety is to Allah, she says.

The unseen becomes visible: all of us, women, yearning for the
divine.

---

[13] Qur'an, Surah Al-Ahzab, 33:35
[14] Qur'an, Surah Al-Mujadila, 58:1

Age 40:

I wake up
in the middle of the night, in Ramadan
A friend sends me a message:
"Every time I hear the verses from Surah Ahzab, I remember
you in Madinah.
Those are literally
your verses."

I sit
with the silence of my own astonishment
I roll around her words in my mouth, feel their lightness
on my tongue
Surah Ahzab.
Madinah.
Your verses.

I finally reply: "My verses.
I love the sound of that."

What I could not bring myself to say at
thirty-nine, at
twenty-seven, at
twenty-one, at
sixteen, I say to myself
now:
from before the time my soul was breathed into a body
not-yet-formed
from before the moment Jibreel brought down those verses
to the Prophet
from before time itself, Allah sent the book for
women, like me
for,
me.
A sign from the unseen for those
who believe in the unseen.

THE FLAMES THAT NEVER STOPPED BURNING
Mariam Ali

When they asked me how I got through
Mondays that were muddled,
Saturdays that shackled,
Tuesdays that were out of place—

what they don't know is:
I didn't.

I had Your soft feathery pages—
the same ones that tasted the salty holy streams,
gushing from my eyes.

     You spoke to me of the expansiveness and beauty around

Sensing I would need genuine company
You let me borrow your ears
each time I needed them.

Burnt by a world untouched by grace,
and unwatered by the rains of mercy,
Your letters gently held me.

     As you listened to the cries of age-old wounds

You saw me oscillating in all my states,
without judgement.

          For the keepers of the book are those in perpetual awe
               How could I not be enlightened
              When I bore within my two hands
                The flames lit by God himself
                   Glory be to Him.

When I ran after the illusion of happiness
and amused myself to death

I came out fragmented and blinded
yet you nursed me day and night

And gave me shelter from the clouds of waswasa

You wrapped your warm reassuring arms around me
Like the loyal companion you were

Do not grieve, do not be saddened.

WHEN SERENITY SPEAKS
Neila Attba

Serenity speaks in the folds of verseful dog-eared page
It speaks in the space between each highlighted letter

It speaks in the rustling sound of a turned leaf
It echoes in the footsteps of children eager to believe

Serenity speaks in the light spilling out of the edges
It speaks in the swirls of golden leaf in the margins

It speaks in gathered whispers wrapping themselves around the
pillars of a mosque
It speaks in the sunlight reflecting off water droplets on freshly
washed hands

Serenity speaks through the delicate verses I hold
Serenity speaks back to them in the gentle whispers I form

Serenity speaks in the folds of a verseful dog-eared page
Its words gather in the ridges left in the clay of creation

COMPANY OF ANGELS

Rania El-Badry

"As for those who say, 'Our Lord is God,' and take the straight path towards Him, the angels come down to them and say, 'Have no fear or grief, but rejoice in the good news of Paradise, which you have been promised. We are your allies in this world and in the world to come, where you will have everything you desire and ask for as a welcoming gift from the Most Forgiving, Most Merciful One.'"
    -   *Qur'an, Surah Al-Fussilat 30-32*

The taxi is a temporary haven,
A solace of lights streaking by you
Between the where you have escaped to
And the whens you have escaped from:

When did your body start to feel alien?
Since when did your skin seek to peel off
And find another home,
Leaving you bare and bleeding?

The road bumps interrupt the knife jabs in your head
And in the deep recesses of your heart,
Drowning out the verses on the radio
That don't break the walls anymore.

But then your guide recites with them,
Marrying his voice to the qari's,
Tugging you from the war zone
To tell you of glad tidings:

For those who believe
And are steadfast,
Do not fear or grieve,
But rejoice in the company

Of angels.

You look at your guide's youth for the first time,
Eyes ahead to roads yet taken,
But pulled through the blazing traffic
By wisps of allies unseen.

Together, let's lay down the weapons
You have wielded against a friend;
Together, wipe off the blood and stitch
With divine thread these slivered pieces.

And when you go back to the place
You have often escaped,
Stick the words on the mirror
For when you have to face yourself.

Remind yourself of this promise
From the One who never breaks His.

LA ILAHA ILLA ANTA SUBHANAKA [15]
Elest Ali

In the belly of a whale.
In the belly of a whale.
In darkness, threefold
a quiet voice rails,

In the depths of the ocean,
in the depths of the night,
a raging mind feeds
on itself without sight.

The gamble with all odds,
the morsel of my doom;
that buried me alive,
in the womb of a tomb.

I call out from this hunger:
no! there is none but You.
Within, without, You are.
And I've wronged myself too.

---

[15] Qur'an, Surah Al-Anbiya, 21:87

BECAUSE ALLAH

Eiman Bushra

Let's take waiting to the desert
sacrifice it and rejoice.
Like Ibrahim rejoiced when Ismael
was replaced by a lamb,
before the knife cut through
the skin of his neck.

This itch for the next thing.
How do we know God will deliver?
When we don't let fear take the wheel
perhaps then He would;
When we bid farewell to lack
nestled in the corner of our heart
echoing the illusion that we don't have

not knowing how another visitor
will be at our door,
and our house had been
pretty lonely before.
But we have a door and we have a house,
and isn't Allah enough for His slave?
And isn't lack a heavy guest to chase?

And the visitors will come,
with an entourage
bearing gifts, baskets laden with blessings!
Because Allah likes it plentiful
because He is,
because Allah likes it grand
because He is,
because Allah likes it
because Allah.

TEN STEPS: RECOVERING THE SOUL
Nusheen Ameenuddin

"When My servants ask about Me: I am near. I respond to one's prayer when they call upon Me."
- *Qur'an, Surah Al-Baqarah 2:186*

"Whoever comes to Me (Allah) walking, I will come to him running."
- *Hadith Qudsi, narrated in Sahih Al-Bukhari 7405*

Step 1: Reach
> Toward the top shelf
> Not distant
> Yet closer than it once seemed

Step 2: Exhale
> Blow off the dust
> Not intended abandonment
> Yet evidence of neglect

Step 3: Unwrap
> Ornate layers that hid jewels of wisdom
> Not to separate
> Yet still a barrier to overcome

Step 4: Hold
> Heavy in both hands
> Not unfamiliar
> Yet still weighty like the mizan[16]

Step 5: Pause
> In stillness, a quiet reflection
> Not hesitation
> Yet memories of unfulfilled niyyah[17] flood in

---

[16] Translated in English as "Scale"
[17] Translated in English as "Intention"

Step 6: Open
	Cardboard spine cracks sharply
	Not supple with regular use
	Yet now apologetically stroked in recognition

Step 7: Inhale
	Breathe in aging parchment, as our ancestors did
	Not a scentless screen
	Yet each verse vibrantly awakening the senses

Step 8: Examine
	Eyes and fingers carefully trace the words our Prophet ﷺ
spoke
	Not merely abstract ideas
	Yet indelibly imprinted on our soul

Step 9: Iqra (Recite/Read)
	"Read in the name of your Lord Who created" [18]
	Not a suggestion
	Yet now the imperative is understood, obeyed

Step 10: Return
	Tears flow in gratitude and relief for this homecoming after
	an extended separation
	Not promised
	Yet always hoped for, asking for the blessing to return
	again and again

---

[18] Qur'an, Surah Al-'Alaq, 96:1

THE TURNING | REFUGE IN THE CAVE

Jesenia Vivas

An honest outpouring,
interlocked fingers.
A purpose unfounded,
a hollowed chest
rising and falling.

Deep breaths rippling unclear.
A rusted, splintered compass.
No guide in my arsenal.

Harrowing fear,
merely existing within a vessel
with no final destination.

Decades of silence,
unanswered inquiries,
warm, half-truths.
Two-seater tables of untouched tarot cards.
Polished, Earth-sung Jasper.
A jagged, delirious conscience.

The Supernatural, with reverence, closes in.

Sound creatures that retinas could never capture.
Feisty wind running marathons through sacred pages.

Mercy.

No more tattered integrity.
Sincere, teary *Allahu Akbars*,
rooted knees relinquished.
A change of pace,
trembling hands open,
blush palms facing upward.

A collapsing

Sujood.

10 seconds,
60 seconds,
an hour.
Unraveling.
Khushu
into
slumber.

Awakened as a slave to
The One.
Tomorrow can carry itself
as I will always seek
refuge in the cave.

ARAFAT

Medina Tenour Whiteman

I trudge through the spine of the house
for the twelve hundredth time today

Labbayk, Allahumma labbayk

smoosh pink aphids from the dogrose's young shoots
let their baby green spines pretend to spike me

Labbayk, Allahumma labbayk

sort through the socks no one wants, pairless, holey,
wonder if here, too, can be a temple, mundane;

Labbayk, Allahumma labbayk

feel the drought in my forehead, ballast hips, scaly eczema palm
swim through the doubting story: shouldn't I be feeling more?

Labbayk, Allahumma labbayk

enter into the shock I've welcomed, be copper filament
or bathe in rock pools after the foaming crash?

Labbayk, Allahumma labbayk

"As long as your heart is connected to Allah"—mutasilan
the silsila thread that salah suggests—"it does not matter where you
are."

Labbayk, Allahumma labbayk

In sujud, this safety that upturns, I sense the waterfall's spray.
O mercy! A moment later: this is only its fragrance, untouched

Labbayk, Allahumma labbayk

Imminence gets you on board (I recall writing); transcendence
makes the craft soar. Grounding, elevating – one presence, cycling.

Labbayk, Allahumma labbayk

Was this where Eve and Adam were reunited? On a hill, dusty-faced,
magnetic reunion driven by thirst and loneliness?

Labbayk, Allahumma labbayk

A silk thread, spooled out from the beginning, perforates the clothes
my being wears, embroiders remembrance. Its cadence sounds

Labbayk, Allahumma labbayk

2:138

Aimen Ahsan Hafeez

"Say, 'Take Allah's color, and who can give a better color than Allah?
Therefore, we worship and submit to Him alone.'"
-   Qur'an, Surah Al-Baqarah 2:138

I was muddied, filthy, all self-stained,
my soul a stagnant murky river I've tried so hard to clear—to no
avail.

My color was shame and shame and shame,
Until I learned that

      If I was to bathe
      I should've bathed in the colors of My Lord
      (How?)

Believe

      For who has better color than He?

      If I was to wash
      (When?)

Always.

      I should've washed in the mercy of My Lord
      Rain, snow, or hail.
      For what is mercy but He?

      If I am to praise,
      And praise I must,

In every condition.

      I should repeat the verses my Lord has taught me,

For how to praise My Lord better than He?

His color is pure and pure and pure
Always everywhere.
My soul is a flowing river now dyed clear.

When I am to die,
I ask that He shroud me not in cloth of earth
please,
in cloth colored divine.

My servant shall have what she has asked for.

HOME

Dalia Rakha

The earth buckles in pain
Pushing against itself in an energy
Unknown
Relentless force
Until it bends, cracks
Jagged and tall
On a mountain face.

Harsh lines
Sharp edges
It cuts even the blue sky
In its stark profile.
The scars of grief
Seldom crumble.

Twisted, torn
Quaking, frail
My heart wrung in a knot so tight,
I don't know if once released,
The creases will unfold.

"My Lord, expand for me my chest" [19]

Fear consumes,
Like flames a golden field

And so I beg,
With every ounce of my being,
For what my brother Musa asked in his time of need:

---

[19] Qur'an, Surah Taaha, 20:25

"My Lord, indeed I am,
For whatever good You would send down to me,
In need" [20]

And indeed Allah delivers:
Letters of rahma so long,
It would take a lifetime
To read the first page.

"Fear not. Indeed, I am with you" [21]

My Lord,
In these letters of Yours
I find solace.
The medicine and the cure.
In the highest of abodes,
No grief, no fear
Mountains crumble
Flames extinguish
Only under Your light.

"My Lord, build for me near You a house" [22]
For home—
Home is a place free of scars.

---

[20] Qur'an, Surah Al-Qasas, 28:24
[21] Qur'an, Surah Taaha, 20:46
[22] Qur'an Surah At-Tahrim, 66:11

AN IDEAL WITNESS
Ahsen Ustaoglu

The heart is enveloped by flesh and blood,
   busied gushing and circulating to keep us
       alive.
Misguidance thickens veils into
   opaque covers, darkening windows of the soul
      until eventually one looks
       but does not see,
until through an embrace of compassion
    you are brought back to the One who Sees All,
      Closer to you than your jugular vein
Who, despite your endless frailty, faltering failures and
    deviations, knocks on the door of your hidden,
      hardened heart again and again.
Ar-Rahim saves a special Mercy for the likes of you,
    regardless of heedless distractions and worldly attachments
      places a heaviness in your bosom,
        a neighbor to the centre of your spirit
to Lovingly Call you Home once more
  so that every teardrop of pain that leaves the eyes can nourish the
garden of your soul,
    so deafened ears can hear the Call of their Creator
     once adversity cuts through the noise of worldly ambition,
and your skin—a blessed barrier between the living and its
surroundings
    gets pricked, slashed and stitched,
      leaving scars of physical suffering, loss, and a
       manifest sign of your moulding
into one who habitually chooses gratitude over grievance.
Rejoice, for glad tidings have been distinctly spelled out—

don't you know your scarred skin will bear witness to your
servitude
                on the Day when Al-Muhyi revives and asks its account?
So spread centaury oil where they entered your subclavian vein
        and fitted an entry port on the day His angels descended
            to cleanse your heart,
            massage it along the curves of the scalpel lines on your chest,
and on the pincushion of your abdomen
                with an elated smile,
                Whisper: bear witness

ONE WHO SUBMITS
Jeri Lee

in a fashion similar to blood
coursing through my veins
i could not see my lifeline
i did not know You were within me

a directionless pull toward
cupped hands whispers to the skies
every bruise revealed a glimpse
a thread of what was before its time

in alkhayr my instinct knew
in yasa my instinct knew
what the naked eye had missed
the natural disposition my fitrah knew

wandering between city walls
echoes travel through dusted alleys
my heart—it travelled too
closer to direction than before

the world's claws split my fine skin
what it has enveloped poured
crimson red ancient rivers flowed
yet the knife did not kill ismaeel

the wound became the eye
what was supposed to end me
unveiled You

subconscious minds remember
the blinded eye becomes anew
catching glimpses of the truth
closer now closer still

the heart tired from its wandering
the eyes in need of more words
the ears in need of more echoes
the veil in its final draw draped over my heart

i submitted in every goodness
in every despair
i submit

BUKHARI'S TONGUE
Shams Alkamil

Tell him that Allah loves him
>Feign your sorrow: for the trumpet blows twice.

Honesty descended from the Skies
>This world is restitched with the fabric of fables.

This worldly life is no more than play and amusement
>Tread honorably on the breast of plated earth.

If Adam's son had a valley full of gold, nothing would fill his mouth except—
>We are only a myriad of clay returned as dust.

Their mothers bore them in hardship and delivered them in hardship
>The mother of my mother of her mother.

When a man dies, his good deeds come to an end except—
>Feign your sorrow: for the trumpet blows twice.

TUUBO/TUUBUU

Asiya Mohamed

we sit in a circle
or perhaps a triangle
our odd crew of three
here, there are no
hierarchies
only repetition
three times is the charm
or perhaps the prayer
god loves odd things
and god must love poetry
we sway
to the rhythm of his verses
language—
a beautiful gift to creation
we sit in a circle,
my mother repeats her mantra
revise, revise, revise,
until your cashar flows
like the tuubo flows
we repeat the verses
until the letters lift off the page
and flow into our bodies
for safekeeping
the image of the flowing tuubo
floats to my mind
when I finally reach
"thumma lam yatuubuu"
of surah buruj, the constellations—
what was god saying
about tap water?
I repeat the verses
until they flow
many years,
many repetitions,

many circles
until I learn
yatuubuu is about tawba
tawba is repentance
a return
to god
a cycle,
circle of its own.
water
adheres to
a cycle
          too.

THE FINAL HALAQA TUN NISA
Mariyyah Sulaiman

We have gathered here for the past ten years
The same length of life
Rasulullah salallahu alaiyhi wa sallam led in Madinah
We have spoken only of Al-Tanzeel
But sister, now I must tell you

    يا أَيُّهَا الْمُدَّثِّرُ [23]
    Ya aayuhal muddaththir
    O thou enveloped in thy cloak

Beyond the benches and rugs lining these walls

When they decide they're through
Pulling out their shovels to bury you

Take the rest

Let the let down
        collapse
        over
        you
Not into you
Take cover
Take heed
What buries fertilizes
        decays
Laying the bed that sows a new day

    قُم فَأَنذِر [24]
    Qum fa anthir
    Arise and warn!

---

[23] Qur'an, Surah Al-Muddathir, 74:1
[24] Qur'an, Surah Al-Muddathir, 74:2

Rise
As if you have never known loss
As if you never left home
As if you have already returned

Hearts under the same moon
Seeing the same dawn
What is held in yours could be held by any
        one
One In A Million crimson roses
        beating
        believing
Not that we understand how we are worthy
Realize it is not about us and rather Allah's mercy

وَلِرَبِّكَ فَاصْبِر [25]
Walirabbika fasbir
And persevere for the sake of your Lord.

No matter how jagged and camouflaged the path appears
How unyielding the earth beneath your feet
Al-Muqeet is the sun guiding seeds through darkness
You
        are cloaked in a light that can never be perceived by the
        eyes of this world

But which illuminates yours
Unwavering tears
        watering sprouts of possibility
 A straining voice
        cradling
        calling
        all that can emerge
Sabr is not a vow of silence
It is the certainty of movement

---

[25] Qur'an, Surah Al-Muddathir, 74:7

moving when all remains still
It is the certainty of roots beneath the soil
anchors we do not witness
Growing in all the places they feared you would
Declaring

هُوَ أَهلُ التَّقوىٰ وَأَهلُ المَغفِرَةِ[26]
Huwa ahlu ttaqwa wa ahlul maghfira.
He [Allah] alone is worthy to be feared and entitled to forgive.

Forget all
but not this final lesson
Of how the pages in your hands began
Pages that have not changed

But testify to your change

Begin
We end with beginning

---

[26] Qur'an, Surah Al-Muddathir, 74:56

THE INHERITORS: POETIC REFLECTIONS ON SURAH AL-MU'MINUN

Syeda Atika Yayha

From time unknown, man sought the truth,
"Who am I?" he asked, with the pride of youth.
He wandered wide, searched land and sky,
while the answer lay close by.

Success, he chased like a fleeting flame,
not knowing his Master had named the aim.
A path laid bare in divine decree—
but blinded by self, he failed to see.

"Qad aflaha al-mu'minoon[27]," the Surah begins,
the believers—successful—free of sins.
Those who bow with humble grace,
and find in prayer their sacred place.

But now—what is prayer but a task?
a duty rushed, a ritual mask.
Where is the heart? The stillness? The plea?
the soul, once yearning, now seeks to flee.

In a world of noise, of slanderous speech,
the successful are those who learn to breach.
The chaos, the clamor, the endless lie—
and turn from gossip as hearts testify.

Where Zakah isn't flaunted to please the crowd,
but a quiet duty—subtle, not loud.
A secret offering between man and Lord,
seeking no fame, no worldly reward.

---

[27] Qur'an, Surah Al-Mu'minun, 23:1

Where modesty isn't mocked but worn with pride,
not a burden, but a shield, a guide.
Where the body obeys, and the gaze looks down,
where dignity is the only crown.

And promises—how lightly they're made and torn!
But the believers guard them, battered and worn.
With trust a jewel they refuse to trade,
in a world where contracts are quickly betrayed.

And again—it ends where it begins,
in prayer, the balm that soothes our sins.
They guard it well, through thick and thin,
a rope to Allah, forever within.

They may be unknown, these souls so true,
but their names are etched where angels flew.
Promised the gardens, the highest place,
Jannatul Firdaus, by Allah's grace.

This is the criterion, the divine test,
not in wealth or titles, but in hearts at rest.
So tell me, soul, what trait will you grow?
Which seed of Jannah will you sow?

BOOK OF YOU
Abdullah Qazi

You are a book being written,
not by your hand, but by a Pen
that moves through you.

The ink is yours:
your choices,
your trembling,
your *ikhtiyār*.

But the parchment?
    His.
The margins?
    His.
The story arcs,
the ellipses where you
      gasp for breath?
All His.

And then there is *The Book*.
Not just ink on a page, but a mirror.
It shows you what you cannot see:
a sea that drowns and delivers,
a storm that tears down the walls you built.
You read it,
and it reads you.

Every *āyah* is a question
you didn't know you were asking.
Laysa kamithlihi shay' [28].
Nothing is like Him.

And yet, here we are——

---

[28] Qur'an, Surah Ash-Shuraa, 42:11: "There is nothing like Him."

a flicker of His light,
a shadow of His Names.
The paradox is the point.

You are free, yet bound.
You are the ink, yet the page.
You are the question, yet the answer.

And this grey you stand in
is not confusion.
It is the colour of *tawakkul*:
the place where His will and yours meet,
like rivers folding into the ocean.

But look around.
This book is not yours alone.
We are all being written,
our stories overlapping, parallel—
a thousand voices in the same breath.
Each of us shaped by different ink,
but written by the same Hand.

I say, burn the veils.
But what if they are not there to hide Him,
but to remind us He is beyond?
Beyond knowing, beyond grasp,
beyond the words we use to name Him.

The veils are not walls.
They are thresholds.
And sometimes, standing at the threshold
is enough.

We dig into ourselves
not because we hold the answers,
but because we are the question.
To know yourself is to know your Lord.

But what if knowing
is not about answers,
but learning to ask
better questions?

The universe is a footnote to your soul.
The stars, the galaxies, the endless sky
all inscribed in the margins
of the Book of You.

And still, you are also the margin—
the quiet edge where the Pen slows,
the breathless pause
before *kun*,
the silence where mercy
prepares to speak.

So let the ink flow.
Let it spill,
let it smudge,
let it stain.
Let it write
you into being,
then erase you.

Let it write
us into being,
then erase us,
then write us again.

We are not the author,
but we are the story.
And the story is His.

When the final page turns,
when the ink dries
and the Pen is lifted,

we will see
the grey was never empty.
It was the canvas,
the space between the lines,
the breath before the Call.

KUN — BE

Huda A. Bakar

And then You breathed your words into the world.
The trees wept, the hills brought down to their knees,
the king's Kaaba stood firm as the rest swirled,
exclaiming: *Surely with hardship comes ease* [29].

And then You called the universe with *Be*—
in mothers' wombs, under the dome of His,
even the fallen, spared not by gravity,
no, not a moment passes—*and it is.*

And then You *swear by figs, olives* [30] and moon,
by heavens and the visitors of night;
a promise of shade in summers of June
and bountiful bounties, seen without sight.

And when we ask about You, *I am near*,
never farther, ever close, ever here.

---

[29] Qur'an, Surah Ash-Sharh, 94:5
[30] Qur'an, Surah At-Tin, 95:1

JUZ' 'AMMA: POEMS BY THE YOUTH

THE QUR'AN
Amira Hamoudi, Age 12

Everything is good about the Qur'an
Surat Al-Kahf, Surat Al-Naba'
All my Iman

A light that guides through the darkest night
A whisper true, a beacon bright

To my heart, the Qur'an is like a treat
Satisfying, pleasant, and sweet

I love the stories and the Shaddah
I love the lessons and the Maddah

It calms my soul when worries start,
A gentle whisper to my heart.

It teaches patience, kind and true,
Guiding all that I say and do.

The Qur'an gives me warmth, guidance, and hope.

QUR'AN POEM
Anaya Mirza, Age 9

The Qur'an has been in a place where all good has come,
The greatness of Arabic now in our hands,
Of all good and bad,
Deeds rising into lush forests,
Our dhikr is sending fruits to our places in Jannah, Inshallah,
Light has touched our birth,
To worship only Allah as our God,
The smile has grown since the Arabic is read,
In beautiful ways,
In front of busy prayer mats,
And in a private room,
The Qur'an is a blessing,
A beautiful, blessing.

ALHAMDULILLAH
Zoya Mirza, Age 12

I am angry.
Rain showers over my head.
Pitter, Patter.
Thunder screams around me.
ZAP.
My heart thumps against my chest.
Thump, thump, thump.
I fiddle with the house keys.
Jingle, jingle, jingle.
I heave open the door.
I drop my bag in the hallway.
Thud.
I bolt up the stairs not caring that I have my shoes on.
Stomp, Stomp, Stomp.
I slam my room's door.
Slam.
I lean my back against it.
Breathe in, Breathe out.
I kick my laundry that I haven't been bothered to fold onto the floor.
I slump myself on the bed.
The colour returns to my cheeks.
Something catches my eyes.
Something Pretty.
The book, navy blue, is lined with golden stripes across it.
I sit up.
I scoot over to the other side of the room, tripping several times over
my laundry.
For a moment, I didn't touch it.
I stared at it.

Finally, my hand reached towards it.
I opened the book.
Light shone onto my face.
Colours danced in front of me as I read the words.
Suddenly, I am no longer angry.
The storm pauses.
I smile.
Alhamdulillah.

IMAGINATION
Lena Elhelbawi, Age 12

You may have a little bit of a struggle but the Qur'an is so amazing it feels like an ice cold popsicle landing on your tongue on a hot, hot summer day,

> you find trees filled with olives,

> > trees filled with figs,

> > > oceans filled with secrets,

> > > mountains filled with caves,

> > ships filled with people,

> animals

and prophets.

The best part about it all is

you get to use your imagination

while you read the beautiful words of Allah

Alhamdulillah.

ACKNOWLEDGMENTS

We wish to first thank House of Amal, especially co-founders Sara Bawany and Amal Kassir, for creating a space for Muslim writers where ideas like this book can incubate. Immense gratitude to the co-collaborators of this project behind the scenes, from gathering to editing and compiling this collection; every step brought with it a sense of barakah, InshaAllah.

Thank you to Imam Dr. Khalid Shahu for his blessed words prefacing this collection, and to Agija M. (@aquarellmuslimah on Instagram) for the beautiful cover art.

This body of work would not be possible without the many amazing contributors, the essence of this project. We are also immensely blessed to partner with Islam in Prison via Al-Furqaan Foundation, to whom 100% of profits from this book's sales will go.

May your words, stories, and experiences guide anyone who picks up this book that may need some extra light in their darker seasons.

ABOUT THE WRITERS

Abdulrahman Taiwo Adedayo is a Nigerian student currently studying Psychology at university. He has a deep passion for poetry and creative writing and aims to share his voice with the world through his writing and poetry. He draws much of his inspiration from nature, personal experiences, inner struggles, human connections, and Islam. He enjoys reading across a wide variety of topics and genres, with the aim of gathering inspiration from all forms of literature.

Elest Ali is a British Muslim writer of Cypriot and Turkish heritage. She studied English Literature (BA) and Comparative Literature (MA) at Kings College London and SOAS. Elest's writing is hell-bent on challenging the tired trope of 'sob stories from the East' and other reductive portrayals; to reclaim the empowered Muslim narrative. She lives in Türkiye where she works as an editor.

Mariam Ali is a passionate poet, storyteller, mother, and Seeker of God and all things good. As a Black Muslim woman, she explores spirituality, racial inequality, and social justice through the lens of her lived experience in the West. Deeply drawn to the power of language, Mariam uses words to illuminate, connect, and inspire positive change in individuals and communities. Writing continues to serve as a vital means of reconnection, thoughtful processing of the world around her, and providing clarity as well as renewed purpose and a deeper understanding of life's complexities.

Shams Alkamil is a Sudanese-American poet. She began writing as a mode of self-expression to then being a three-time Pushcart Prize nominee. Alkamil's work speaks of the immigrant experience, Islam, and womanhood. Her work has appeared in *Four Way Review*, *Mizna*, *The Ana*, *Torch Literary Arts*, and more. Alkamil's second book, "When Time is Circular", was published in June 2024.

Nusheen Ameenuddin is a Midwestern-raised, Indian American Muslim woman who has been a practicing pediatrician for 20 years and hijabi since her senior year of high school. She just published her first children's book, "Are Cats Muslim?" in Ramadan 2025 through Little Hibba and her second children's book on Dhul Hijjah is currently in the illustration stage. She is most inspired to write to share the beauty of Islam.

Neila Attba is a 22-year-old Algerian woman, and a second-year master's student at the Sorbonne in Paris. She has an English major but specializes in Literature, specifically Postcolonial Literature where she focuses on Anglophone Arab Literature. She has previously worked on Soundscapes and Archives in Arab-American women's novels, and currently working on a Arab-British/Irish women's plays on Iraq.

Huda A. Bakar writes to trace the way we live, feel, and make sense of our experiences. She appreciates the art of noticing—of pausing, paying attention, and letting meaning unfold gently over time. Outside of writing, she works at an experiential agency and finds grounding in travel, suhbah, and time in nature.

Mahmoodulhasan Bhaiyat is a Toronto-based and raised hafiz, poet, photographer, and collector of whatever fits his fancy—a rock here, an acorn there. With a BSc in kinesiology, he is now pursuing a master's in speech language pathology. His favorite genre of poetry is classical Arabic poetry, the likes of al-Mutanabbi and Abu Firas al-Hamdani.

Ikram Bouhedda is a student of Islamic sciences and a practicing civil engineer in California. She admires poetry genres in reflection from knowing to loving Allah and the Beloved ﷺ through the depths of divine blessings. When she's not working or studying, Ikram enjoys photography, hiking, and creating.

Eiman Bushra is a Sudanese poet and spoken word artist who has lived in different parts of the Muslim world. She is a Nile University of Nigeria graduate, with a Bachelor's of English Studies with Honors. She is a breakthrough faith coach, helping mainly Muslims break through limiting beliefs and increasing certainty and good expectations of Allah to receive their already answered dua'as. Eiman is also a former House of Amal 2025 Resident. She is currently writing her debut poetry collection, titled, "A Feast of Light."

Warren Clementson has featured in *Erro Press, Thawra, From Whispers to Roars, Rowayat* and the *Threads of Palestine Anthology*. He resides in the UK.

Rania El-Badry is an American-Egyptian writer and educator with an MFA in Creative Writing. She spends her time largely obsessing over and meditating on the power of words and stories, and their ability to shape ideas, identities, beliefs, and acts of resistance.

Fatima ElKalay is a poet, translator, fiction writer, and artist. She is the Managing Editor at Rowayat, a literary journal committed to championing underrepresented voices across the Arab world, SWANA, and the Global South. A long-standing poetry editor with the magazine, she has been writing poetry since childhood. Fatima's work—spanning translation, short fiction, and collaborative collections—has appeared in *Rusted Radishes, ArabLit Quarterly, The Markaz Review*, and others. She is drawn to reflective themes that explore language, memory, philosophy, and the human condition.

Aimen Ahsan Hafeez is a Pakistani-American poet, currently residing in Austin. She is a lover of cool rocks, heart-shaped things, and literary expression. She believes that words are a gift from God. You can find her on Substack: @wordmosaics.

Hassan Hussein Abdul Hakim is a lyrical poet, spiritual essayist, and spoken word artist whose work explores the intersection of Revelation, revolution, and identity. Rooted in the Ahl al-Sunnah tradition, his poetry reflects a deep love for the Qur'an, the Prophet Muhammad ﷺ and the responsibility of language. His writing has been featured in literary journals and performed in sacred and activist spaces alike. Hassan's work seeks to bridge personal yearning with prophetic clarity, and to illuminate the divine architecture beneath the world's noise.

Sumayyah Hussein is a writer, English teacher, and mother of two teenage girls. She was born and raised in Toronto, Canada, and currently lives in Alexandria, Egypt. She has several picture books and middle grade novels published with Ruqaya's Bookshelf, an independent Muslim publisher based in Canada. Two of her recent publications are *Sido's Prayer Beads*, a picture book about memory loss, and *Pushed to the Back*, the sequel to her previous middle grade novel, *Stuck in the Middle*.

Zana Ishak is a Singapore-based writer who graduated in creative writing and now teaches English. Poetry is her primary genre, and the poem she returns to most is "A Letter from a Stupid Woman" by Nizar Qabbani. She is drawn to poems and prose that reflect slices of everyday life and speak to war, love, and faith. When not writing, Zana unwinds by watching sitcoms with a cup of tea.

Hajera Khaja is a writer, editor, and creative writing teacher. Her short stories and personal essays have been published in literary magazines, including *The Ex-Puritan, The Humber Literary Review, Joyland,* and elsewhere. She is an editor at Ruqaya's Bookshelf and runs creative writing programs for Muslim women. She has completed a short story collection and has several other projects she is tinkering with – some picture book stories, a memoir about her writing journey, and a speculative novel.

Umar Latif is a student of accounting living in Pakistan who has just recently started writing poetry. He's always had interests in rigorous, logical things like chess or maths. Poetry is the complete antithesis of all his other hobbies but surprisingly, he finds solace in the abstract nature of it. Mostly having read older lyrical poems by Wordsworth, Poe, Frost, he ends up adapting some elements of their writing in the pursuit of his own voice.

Jeri Lee, a former private scribbler from London, found the courage to share her writing last year, a blessing she recognises as from Allah (SWT). Becoming Muslim has led her on a path of increased light and purpose, shaping work rooted in lived experience and faith. Fiction is currently her favourite; she is working on a novel, a poetry collection, and her Substack newsletter, while also contributing non-fiction and informative writing to The Thinking Muslim Substack. She hopes her words may serve as a tool for goodness and empowerment, bringing healing or encouragement, as the words of others have settled gently in her heart.

Asiya Mohamed is a Somali-American living in Buffalo, New York. She holds degrees in French Literature and Islamic Studies. She is an avid reader, a patron of the arts, and enjoys community building.

Abdullah Qazi is a tālib-e-'ilm (a student of knowledge). Writing, for him, is a form of catharsis, a way to reflect, to release, and to return. Sometimes, a few sounds or verses from the Book of the Cosmos, the Book of the Divine, or the Book of Us arrive uninvited—and they shake him, and they shape him. For him, poetry helps in reaching places where something within needs support or light.

Dalia Rakha is an environmental engineer and water scientist, passionate about alleviating human health impacts from contamination, especially in drinking water. She had the privilege of attending Tayseer Seminary, where she found a deep connection between the study of the natural world and that of the Creator. Her writing often includes natural systems as reminders of God's mercy, perfection, and love. She enjoys the transformative nature of poetry and its ability to turn something painful into something beautiful. Outside of writing, Dalia enjoys running, painting, reading, and experimenting in the kitchen.

Mariyyah Sulaiman is a poet, painter, and paper crafter from New York. Much of her work is inspired by her Guyanese heritage, interest in art history, and love for nature. She has a BA in International Studies and an MA in Economics. Mariyyah works in the public sector with a focus on immigrant communities and local commerce. In both her art and professional career, Mariyyah seeks to do work that connects people, expands perspectives, and builds new opportunities.

Ahsen Ustaoglu is a postdoctoral research scientist based at University of Cambridge with roots from Istanbul, and a poet at heart. Her research on gastrointestinal disease, and opinion pieces have been published in peer-reviewed science journals including Nature Reviews. She trained as an editor for United European Gastroenterology Journal and hosted the journal's podcast for two years, and currently runs her own podcast Coffee Break Science. She survived an aggressive, hereditary form of breast cancer at the age of 27, while working in cancer research, and her creative writing is deeply influenced by this experience which she recently started sharing on Substack: Thoughts of a Muslim Scientist.

Jesenia Vivas is a Puerto Rican and Honduran writer, educator, and multidisciplinary artist. She holds a BA in English and is the founder of Notas de Nibras. Her work blends poetry, creative nonfiction, and reflection to explore faith, language, memory, and embodiment. Rooted in Islam, her writing moves with care and intimacy, attending to questions of devotion, identity, and becoming. Jesenia teaches first grade and writes at the intersection of pedagogy and spiritual practice, centering tenderness, ethical attention, and the quiet work of transformation.

Medina Tenour Whiteman is a British-American Muslim writer, poet and singer based near Granada, Spain. She's the author of the poetry collection "Love is a Traveller and We Are Its Path", "Huma's Travel Guide to Islamic Spain", and "The Invisible Muslim: Journeys Through Whiteness and Islam." Her work has appeared on BBC Radio, Critical Muslim, Sacred Footsteps, Amaliah, Rowayat, and other platforms, and been anthologised in "A Kaleidoscope of Stories", "The Ordinary Chaos of Being Human", and "Meandering: Art, Ecology and Metaphysics." She is the cofounder of The Muslim Writers' Salon.

Syeda Atika Yahya is an Indian Muslim mother of four and a self-published author of *Allah Made You Beautiful* and *Allah Loves You*. She writes to inspire faith, heal hearts, and nurture Islamic values in families through reflective storytelling and poetry.

Lena Elhelbawi is 12 years old living in North Carolina with her mom, dad and two sisters. She is a 6th grader who is excited to have her first ever poem published in a book.

Amira Hamoudi is 12 years old.

Anaya Mirza is 9 years old. She has recently started to pick up the Quran again, not letting it catch dust on the shelf. She finds its stories fascinating, especially relating the Prophet's life to her. Mostly, the translation is a book for her, that fits right in her brain. The soul of the Prophet's and their wives interests her a lot, especially the way the Quran settles it.

Zoya Mirza is 12 years old. She loves writing poems that turn emotions into stories. She enjoys using sounds, feelings, and little details to bring moments to life. Writing helps her understand herself better, especially when she is feeling big emotions like anger or joy. Zoya also loves reading—especially the Quan, which gives her peace and inspiration.

ABOUT THE CONTRIBUTORS

Imam Dr. Khalid Shahu is the Imam of the Muslim Community of Knoxville (MCK) as well as the founder of Apex Mosque in North Carolina, for which he served as an Imam from 2010-2020. Dr. Shahu earned his B.A. in Arabo-Hispanic Linguistics & Literatures, his M.A.s in Arabo-Hispanic Linguistics and in Philosophy of Language, and his Ph.D. in Sociology of Language, with a concentration on Language Policy & Planning in Post-Colonial North African Countries. Dr. Shahu has served as a foreign language instructor, lecturer of Arabic & Spanish languages and cultures, and as a Teaching Assistant Professor of Arabic. He is widely published on topics around Qur'an and language, and he is working on other publications through his extensive community projects.

Agija M is an artist whose practice is rooted in Islamic art, exploring spirituality, memory, and the human condition through visual language. Alongside her personal artistic work, she is active as a book illustrator and arts teacher, engaging with storytelling, education, and the transmission of artistic tradition. Her work balances personal reflection with collective meaning, inviting viewers into spaces of contemplation, tenderness, and shared humanity. You can find her work on Instagram: @aquarellmuslimah

ABOUT THE EDITORS

Sara Farhat is a Lebanese-Canadian educator and craft enthusiast in Toronto, with a deep love for STEM, nature, and all things handmade. Her writing draws inspiration from immersing herself in nature, taking notice of life's fine details, and Arabic poetry. Beyond the page, you can find her reading, hiking, creating art in cafes, crocheting, and taking photography. You can find her work on Instagram (@smilesofsunshine).

Ahmed Ayoub is a product designer and writer, having self-published his debut poetry collection "Kintsugi Through a Kaleidoscope." His poetry (and longer works) have been featured in *Rowayat Literary Journal, ILLUMINATION, Late Fee Magazine,* and *UX Collective.* He resides in the NYC area and you can find him at bookstores, tea shops, record stores, or online @ayoubience.

Tehreem Khalid is a Pakistani-Canadian writer who has been published in *Threads of Palestine Anthology* and *The Madrid Review* magazine. She works as a radiation therapist treating patients with cancer. She understands the power of words and is keen to share her worldview through inked pages. When she isn't immersed in a book or a TV show, she can be found hanging out with her cats, swimming, learning a new hobby, or exploring the Canadian Rockies. You can find her work online on Instagram @tehreem.thepoet.

Eiman Bushra is a Sudanese poet and spoken word artist who has lived in different parts of the Muslim world. She is a Nile University of Nigeria graduate, with a Bachelor's of English Studies with Honors. She is a breakthrough faith coach, helping mainly Muslims break through limiting beliefs and increasing certainty and good expectations of Allah to receive their already answered dua'as. Eiman is also a former House of Amal 2025 Resident. She is currently writing her debut poetry collection, titled, "A Feast of Light."

Mariam Ali is a passionate poet, storyteller, mother, and Seeker of God and all things good. As a Black Muslim woman, she explores spirituality, racial inequality, and social justice through the lens of her lived experience in the West. Deeply drawn to the power of language, Mariam uses words to illuminate, connect, and inspire positive change in individuals and communities. Writing continues to serve as a vital means of reconnection, thoughtful processing of the world around her, and providing clarity as well as renewed purpose and a deeper understanding of life's complexities.

Sara Bawany MFA, MSSW, is an award-winning poet, author, and clinical social worker based in Austin, TX. She is the author of two poetry books: *(w)holehearted: a collection of poetry and prose* and *Quarter Life Crisis*, as well as the curator and editor for *Threads of Palestine Anthology*. She manages her own mental health practice and is the Co-Founder and Lead Writing Instructor of House of Amal, a virtual school of that focuses on nurturing spiritually centered craft and community for its Muslim writers. You can learn more about her work at www.sarabawany.com.

ABOUT HOUSE OF AMAL

Founded in July 2020, House of Amal is a dynamic foster home for the creative Muslim writer seeking craft and community. We believe that every Muslim creative deserves space to develop their craft, find their voice, and connect with a like-minded faith-centered writing community, while building bridges between Muslim writers and the broader literary world.

House of Amal's teaching philosophy centers on hands-on learning through craft instruction, writing studios, generative workshops, and service-oriented projects. We offer a robust 12-month writing residency curriculum developing technical skill and artistic voice through intensive training in poetry, prose, and storytelling. Our thriving membership program provides exclusive access to monthly book clubs, generative workshops, community open mics, and notable visiting writers, supported by mentorship and feedback.

From humble beginnings, House of Amal has now published two community anthologies showcasing Muslim creative expression, with 100% of the profits going to charity.

In line with this, 100% of the proceeds of this book will go to Islam in Prison (www.islaminprison.org), a division of Al-Furqaan Foundation (www.furqaan.org). We urge you to buy this book directly from its source and/or from independent local booksellers.

May Allah accept from you and from us.

www.ingramcontent.com/pod-product-compliance
Lightning Source LLC
Chambersburg PA
CBHW040125150726
48005CB00015B/2369